Shifting in Keys for Cello

Book One:

Keys of C, G, D, F, and B♭

by Cassia Harvey

CHP244

©2014 by C. Harvey Publications All Rights Reserved.

www.charveypublications.com - print books & free sheet music blog
www.learnstrings.com - PDF downloadable books & chamber music

C Major Scale

Cassia Harvey

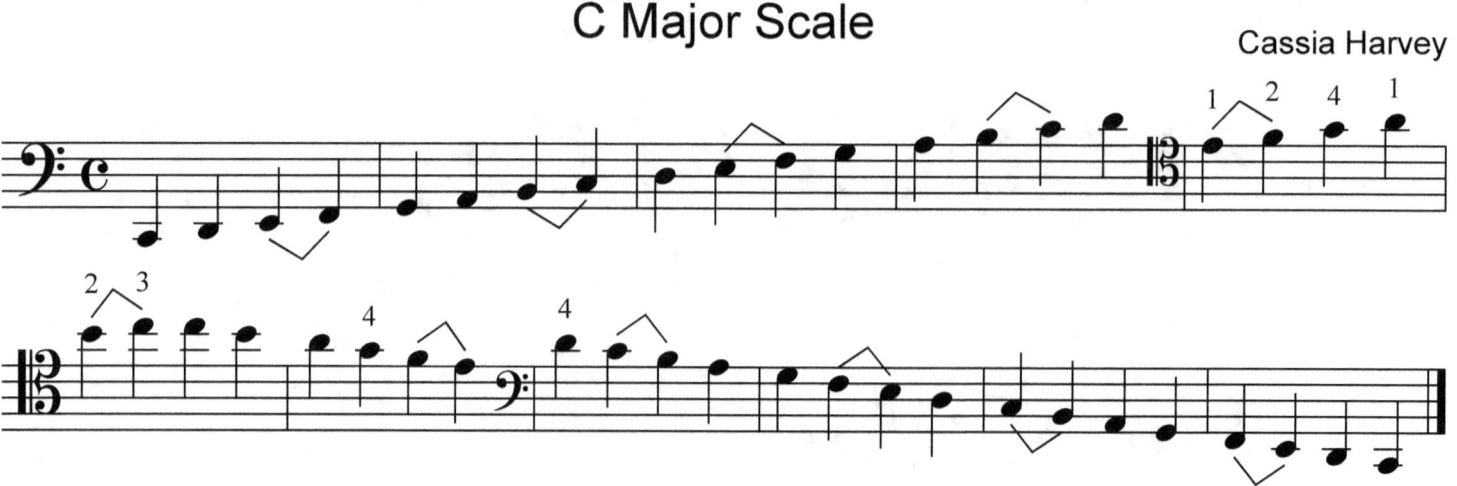

The half steps in C major are between E and F, and between B and C.
All of the other spaces between the notes in C major are whole steps.

©2014 C. Harvey Publications All Rights Reserved.

Shifting in Keys for Cello, Book One

C Major Study No. 1

©2014 C. Harvey Publications All Rights Reserved.

C Major Study No. 2

Shifting in Keys for Cello, Book One

C Major Study No. 3

C Major Study No. 4

Shifting in Keys for Cello, Book One

C Major Study No. 5

C Major Study No. 6

C Major Study No. 7

Shifting in Keys for Cello, Book One

C Major Study No. 9

G Major Scale

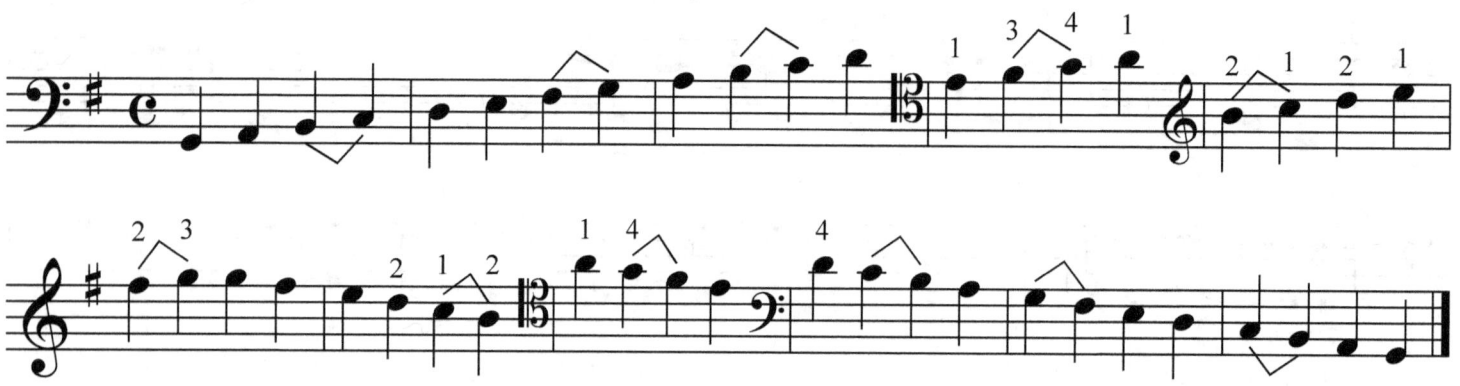

The half steps in G major are between B and C, and between F♯ and G.
All of the other spaces between the notes in G major are whole steps.

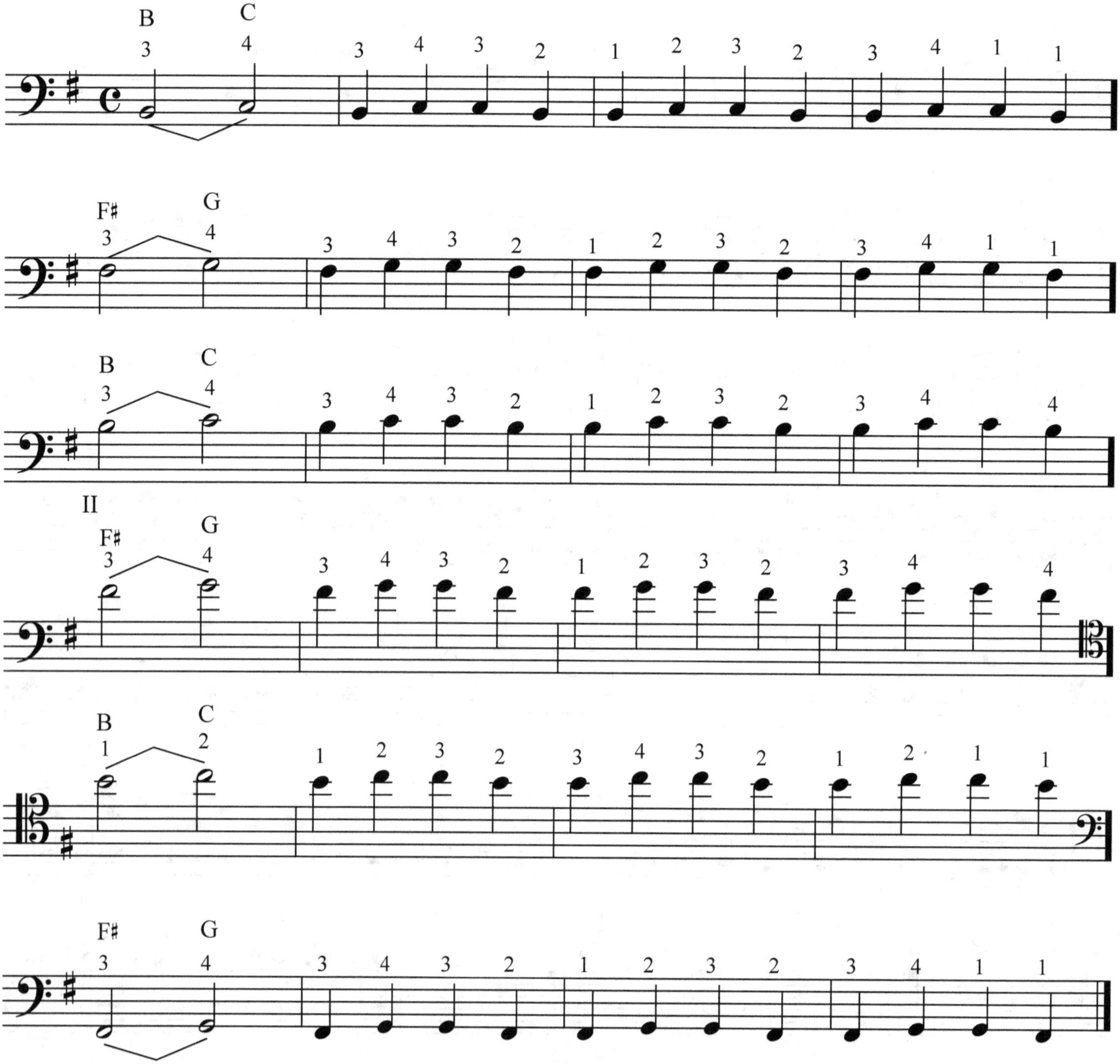

©2014 C. Harvey Publications All Rights Reserved.

Shifting in Keys for Cello, Book One

G Major Study No. 1

©2014 C. Harvey Publications All Rights Reserved.

G Major Study No. 2

Shifting in Keys for Cello, Book One

G Major Study No. 3

©2014 C. Harvey Publications All Rights Reserved.

G Major Study No. 4

Shifting in Keys for Cello, Book One

G Major Study No. 5

©2014 C. Harvey Publications All Rights Reserved.

G Major Study No. 6

Shifting in Keys for Cello, Book One

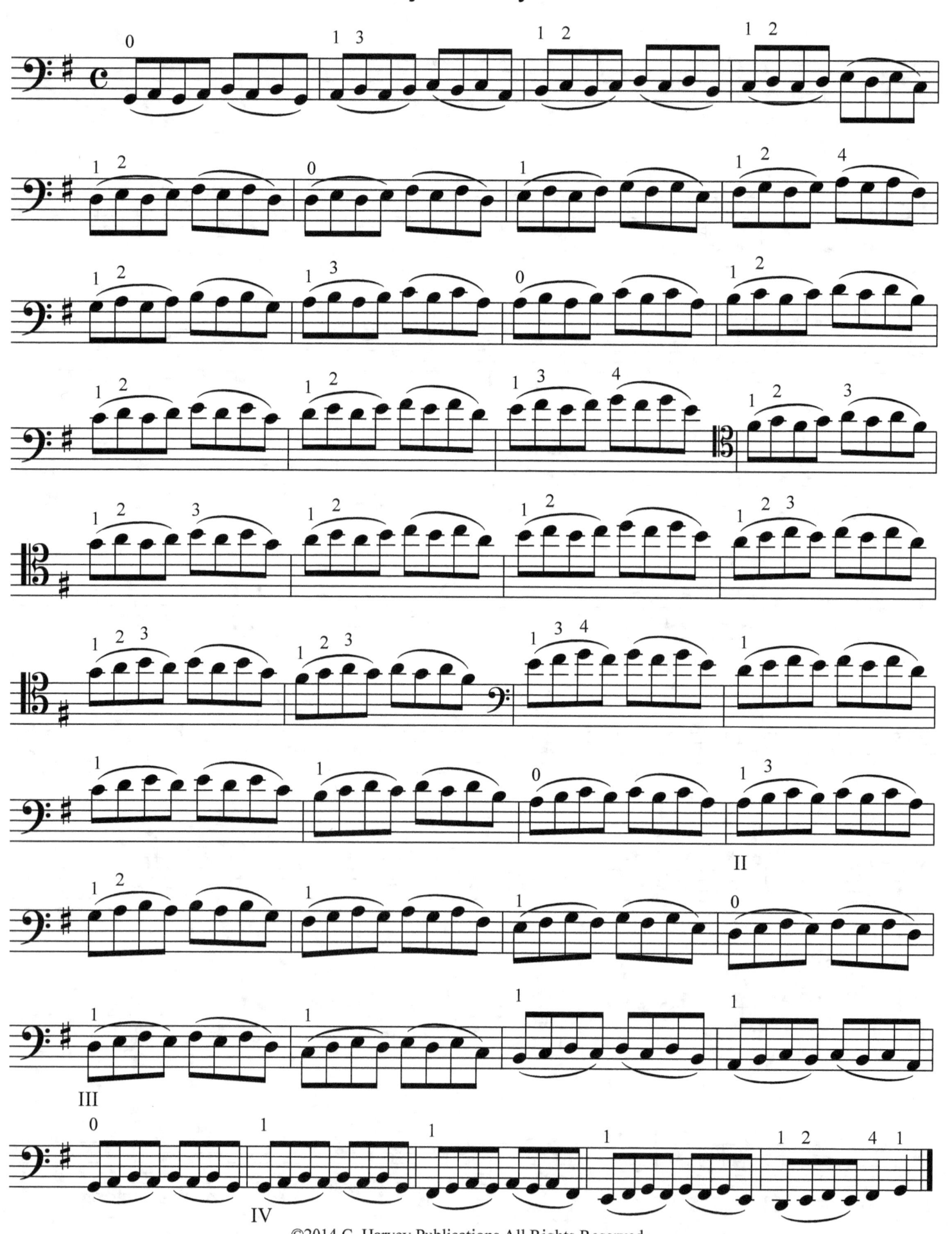

G Major Study No. 7

G Major Study No. 8

G Major Study No. 9

D Major Scale

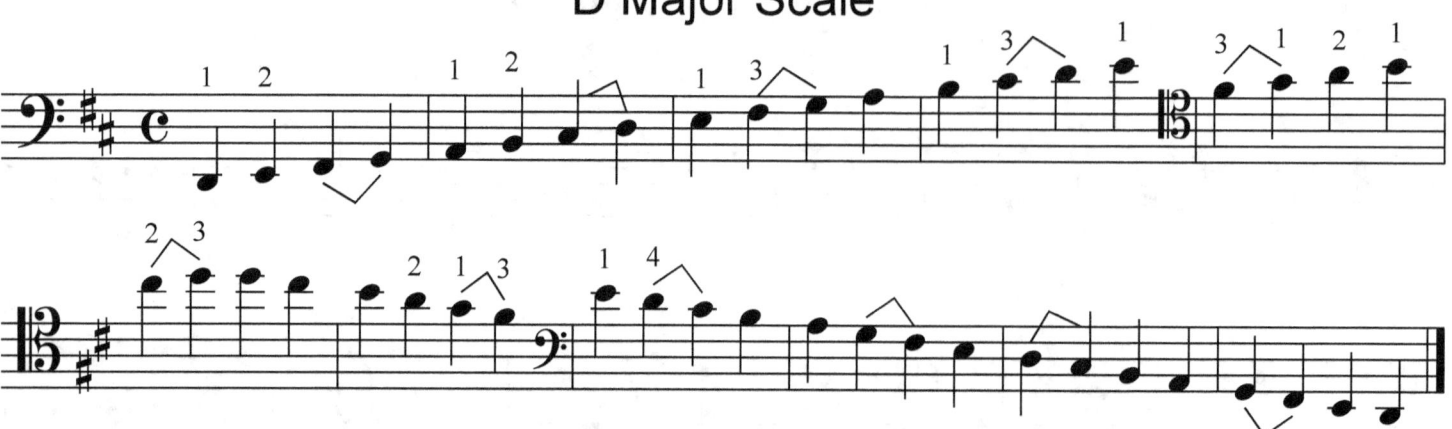

The half steps in D major are between F♯ and G, and between C♯ and D.
All of the other spaces between the notes in D major are whole steps.

©2014 C. Harvey Publications All Rights Reserved.

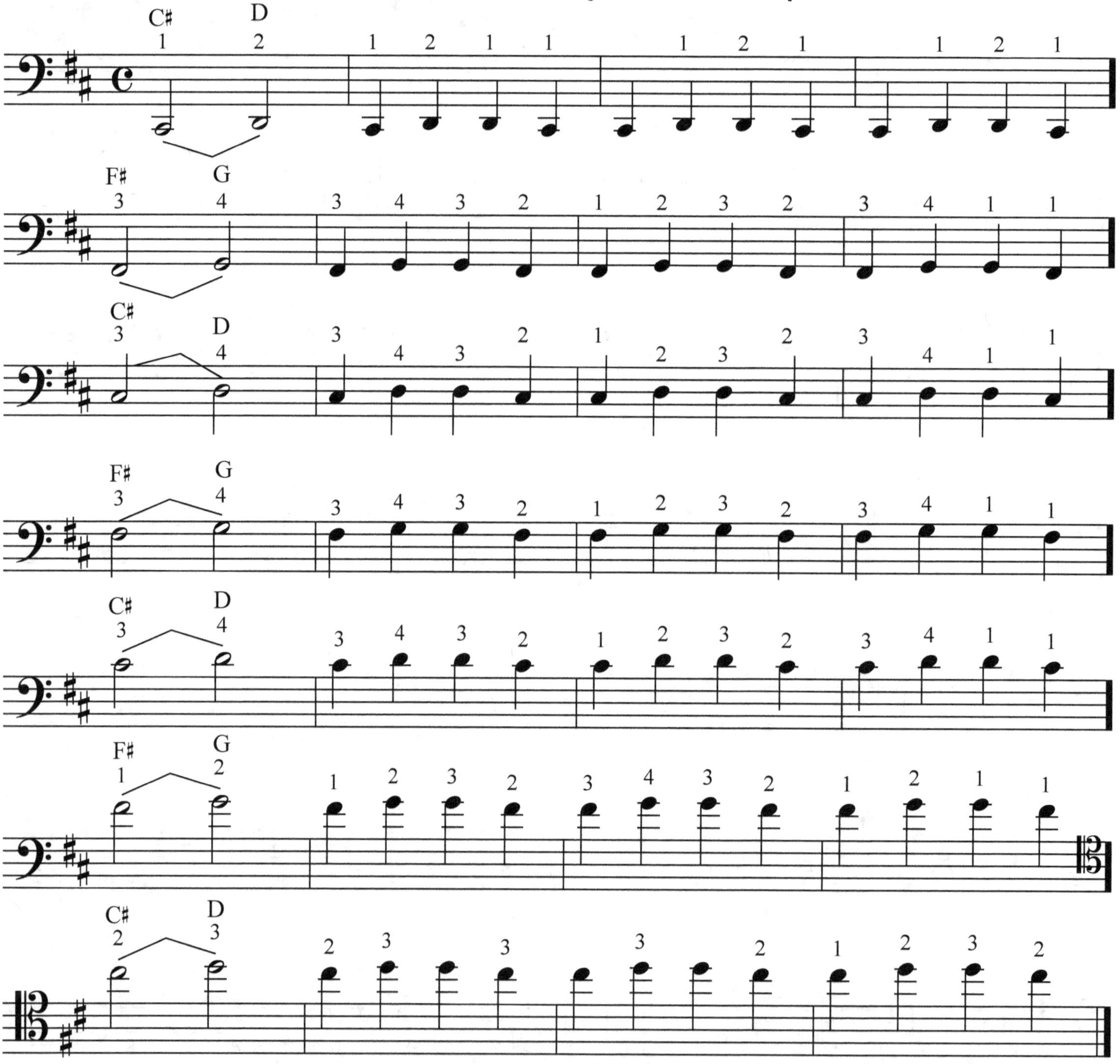

D Major Study No. 1

D Major Study No. 2

D Major Study No. 3

D Major Study No. 4

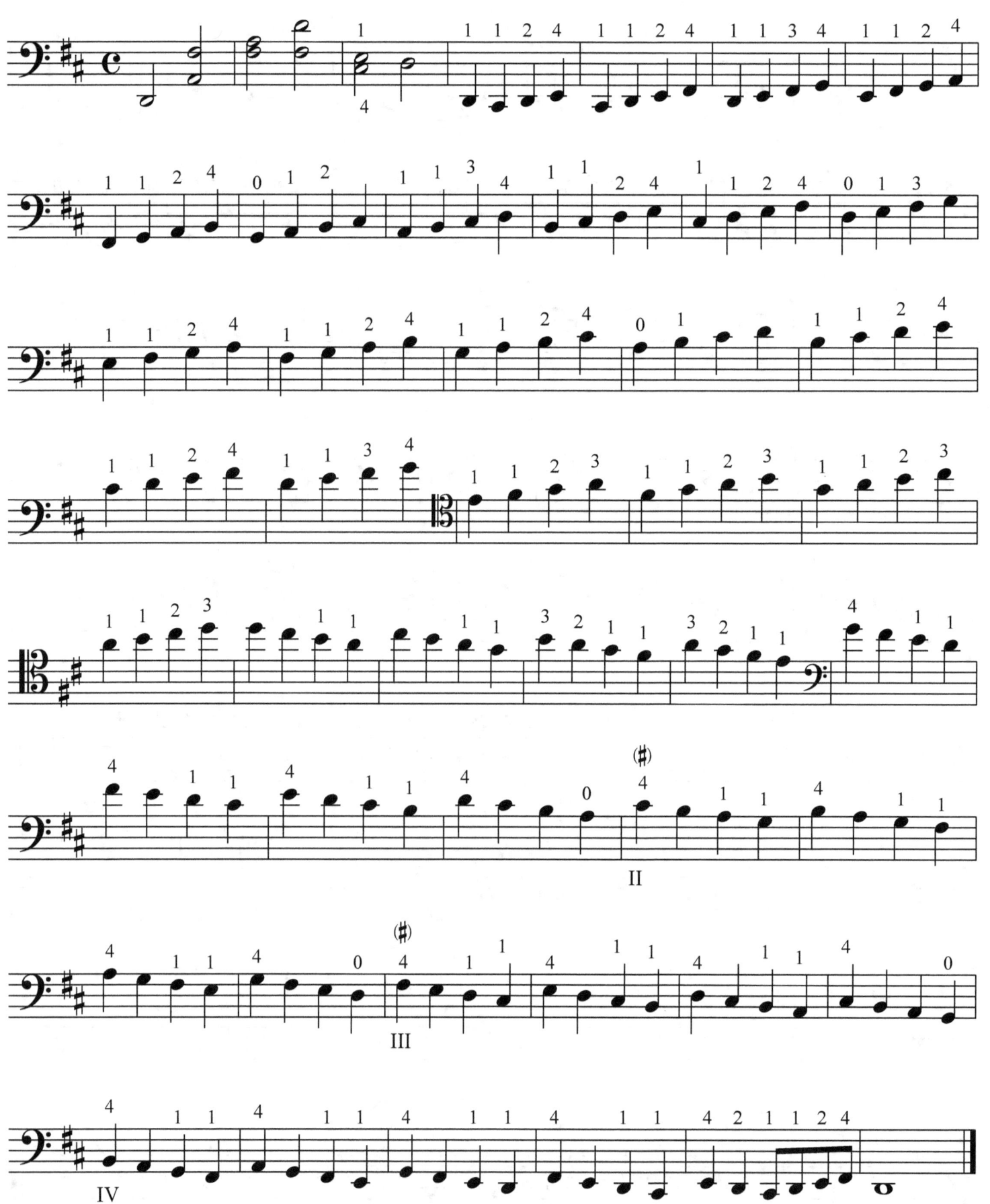

D Major Study No. 5

D Major Study No. 6

Shifting in Keys for Cello, Book One

D Major Study No. 7

©2014 C. Harvey Publications All Rights Reserved.

D Major Study No. 8

D Major Study No. 9

F Major Scale

**The half steps in F major are between A and B♭, and between E and F.
All of the other spaces between the notes in F major are whole steps.**

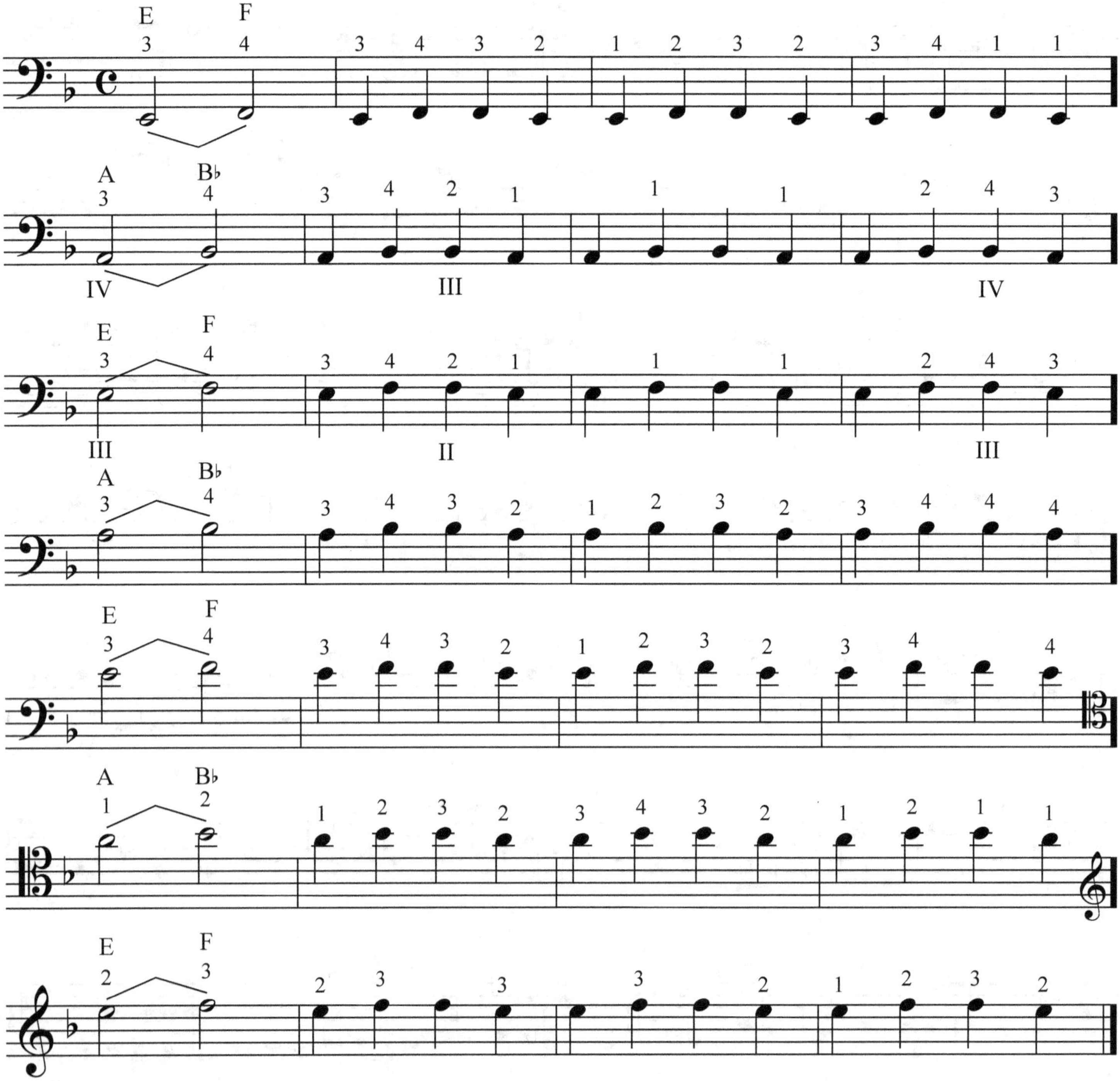

Shifting in Keys for Cello, Book One

F Major Study No. 1

©2014 C. Harvey Publications All Rights Reserved.

F Major Study No. 2

Shifting in Keys for Cello, Book One

©2014 C. Harvey Publications All Rights Reserved.

F Major Study No. 3

F Major Study No. 4

Shifting in Keys for Cello, Book One

©2014 C. Harvey Publications All Rights Reserved.

F Major Study No. 5

F Major Study No. 6

F Major Study No. 7

F Major Study No. 8

F Major Study No. 9

Shifting in Keys for Cello, Book One

©2014 C. Harvey Publications All Rights Reserved.

B♭ Major Scale

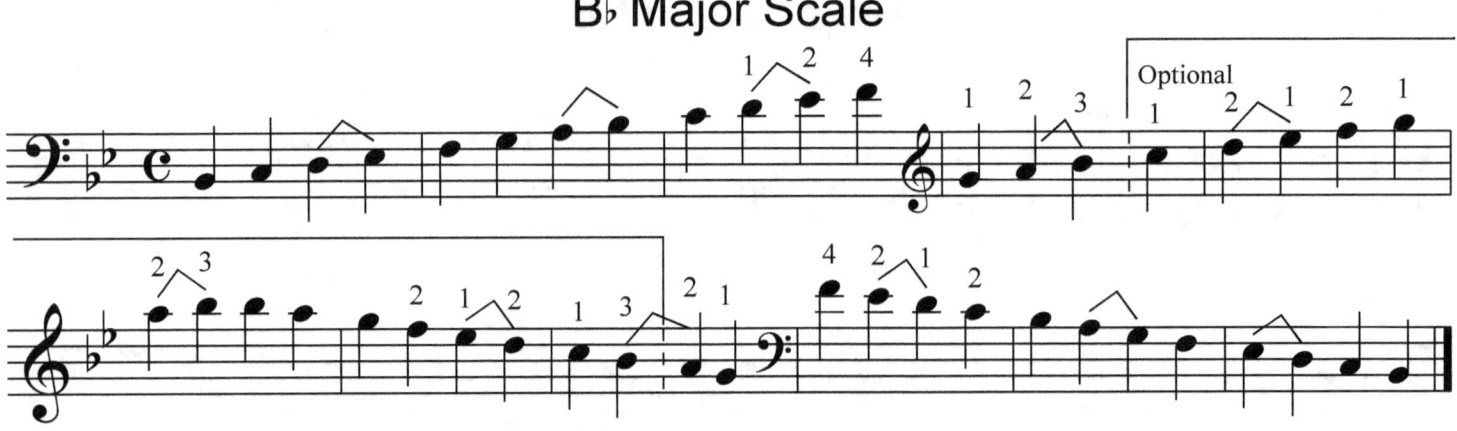

The half steps in B♭ major are between D and E♭, and between A and B♭.
All of the other spaces between the notes in B♭ major are whole steps.

©2014 C. Harvey Publications All Rights Reserved.

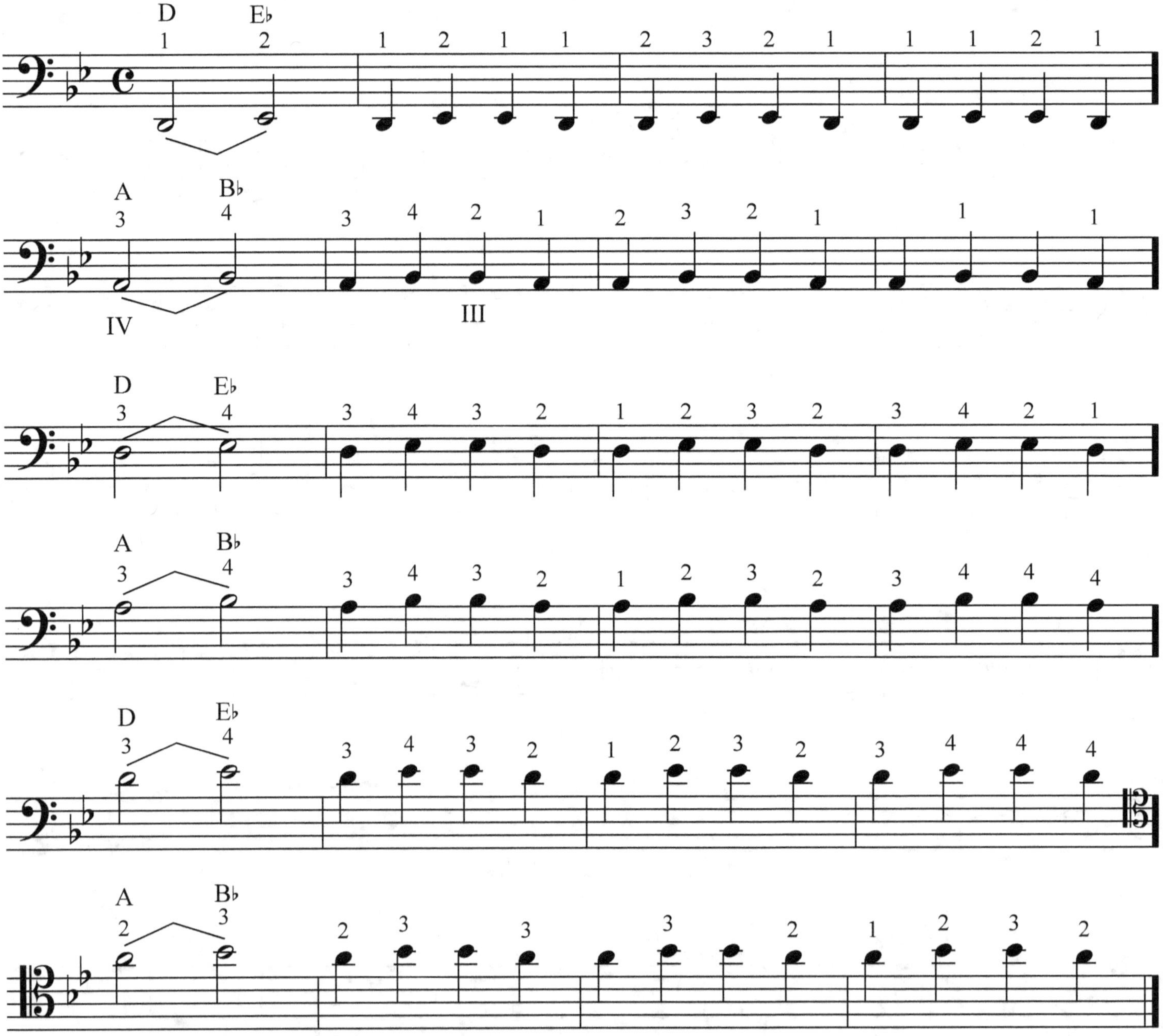

Shifting in Keys for Cello, Book One

B♭ Major Study No. 1

©2014 C. Harvey Publications All Rights Reserved.

B♭ Major Study No. 2

Shifting in Keys for Cello, Book One

B♭ Major Study No. 3

B♭ Major Study No. 4

B♭ Major Study No. 5

B♭ Major Study No. 6

Shifting in Keys for Cello, Book One

B♭ Major Study No. 7

B♭ Major Study No. 8

B♭ Major Study No. 9

Shifting in Keys for Cello, Book One

©2014 C. Harvey Publications All Rights Reserved.

Also available from www.charveypublications.com: CHP356
Learning Three-Octave Scales on the Cello

Part One: Learning the Major Scales

C Major Scale

Cassia Harvey

©2019 C. Harvey Publications All Rights Reserved.

www.ingramcontent.com/pod-product-compliance
Lightning Source LLC
Chambersburg PA
CBHW051424070526
44584CB00023B/3573